Table of Contents

rourkeeducationalmedia.com

Can you find these words?

battle

fighters

independence

visit

The Alamo

A symbol stands for an idea.

The Alamo is in
San Antonio, Texas.

It is a symbol of **independence**.
It is a symbol of freedom.

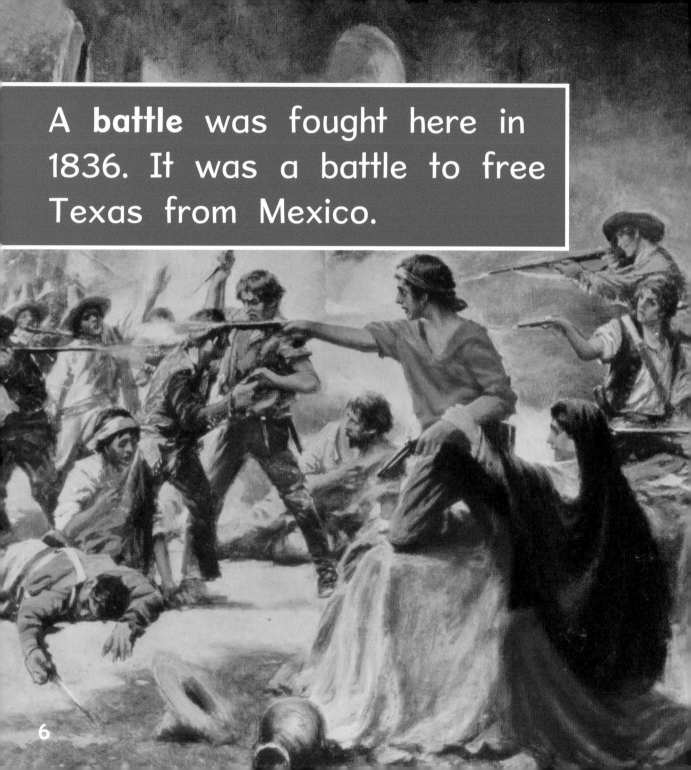

A **battle** was fought here in 1836. It was a battle to free Texas from Mexico.

HERE LIE THE REMAINS
OF
TRAVIS, CROCKETT, BOWIE
AND
OTHER ALAMO HEROES
THE ARCHDIOCESE
OF SAN ANTONIO

ORMERLY BURIED
N THE SANCTUARY
OF THE OLD
SAN FERNANDO
CHURCH

ERE
MAF
R.I.P.

EXHUMED
JULY 28, 1936.
EXPOSED TO
PUBLIC VIEW
FOR A YEAR.
MAF

Texas lost the battle.

TRAVIS   CROCKE

But they were ready to fight again.

ERR **8** GEORGE C. KIMBLE · WILLIAM P. KING · JOHN G. KING · WILLIAM IRVINE LEW
CKINNEY · ELIEL MELTON · THOMAS R. MILLER · WILLIAM MILLS · ISAAC MIL

"Remember the Alamo!" the **fighters** said.

J. LIGHTFOOT · JONATHAN L. LINDLEY · WILLIAM LINN · TORIBIO D. LOSOYA · GEORG
ARD F. MITCHASSON · EDWIN T. MITCHELL · NAPOLEON B. MITCHELL · ROBERT B. MC

9

Texas won! It gained its independence from Mexico.

UNITED STATES
OF AMERICA

TEXAS

MEXICO

GULF OF MEXICO

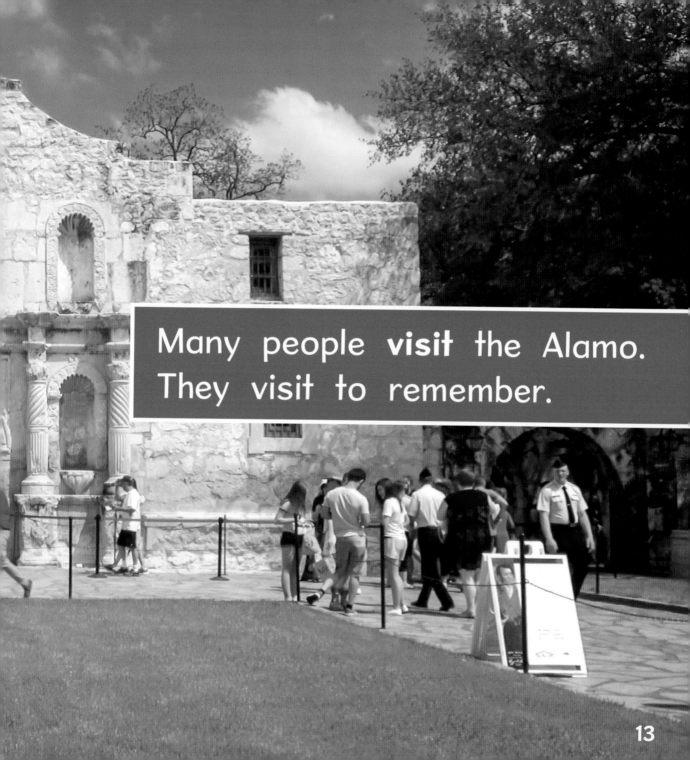

Many people **visit** the Alamo.
They visit to remember.

Did you find these words?

A **battle** was fought here in 1836.

"Remember the Alamo!" the **fighters** said.

It is a symbol of **independence**.

Many people **visit** the Alamo.

Photo Glossary

 **battle** (BAT-uhl): A fight between people or armies.

 **fighters** (FITE-urhs): People who engage in an argument or battle.

 **independence** (in-di-PEN-duhns): Freedom, or the state of being independent.

 **visit** (VIZ-it): To go somewhere and spend time with people or exploring a place.

Index

About the Author

K.A. Robertson is a writer and editor who enjoys learning about the history of the United States. She especially likes to read about the people who were part of history, such as the famous Davy Crockett, who died at the fall of the Alamo.

© 2019 Rourke Educational Media

www.rourkeeducationalmedia.com

PHOTO CREDITS: Cover, p10: ©400tmax; p2,6,14,15: ©Library of Congress; p2,8,14,15: ©Alex Stork; p2,4,14,15: ©laddio1234; p2,12,14,15: ©CrackerClips; p3: ©asiseeit; p7: ©Pgiam

Edited by: Keli Sipperley
Cover and interior design by: Rhea Magaro-Wallace
Interior Layout by: Corey Mills

Library of Congress PCN Data
The Alamo / K.A. Robertson
(Visiting U.S. Symbols)
ISBN 978-1-64369-061-2 (hard cover)(alk. paper)
ISBN 978-1-64369-078-0 (soft cover)
ISBN 978-1-64369-208-1 (e-Book)
Library of Congress Control Number: 2018955839

Printed in the United States of America, North Mankato, Minnesota